Artists Through the Ages

Camille Pissarro

Alix Wood

WINDMILL BOOKS

New York

Published in 2015 by **Windmill Books**, An Imprint of Rosen Publishing
29 East 21st Street, New York, NY 10010

Editor for Alix Wood Books: Eloise Macgregor
Designer: Alix Wood

Photo Credits: Cover, 1 © Tate Britain/Yorck Project; 3, 4, 5, 12 © Shutterstock;
4 top, 9 top © public domain; 6-7, 13, 15, 16-17, 23 © nga/Mr and Mrs Paul Mellon;
8 © Thyssen-Bornemisza Museum; 9 bottom © Musée Guimet/Dalbera; 10-11 © Artothek;
14 © Yorck project; 20 © nga/Ailsa Mellon Bruce Collection; 22, 29 © nga/Rosenwald
Collection; 25 © Van Gogh Museum; 26-27 © nga/Chester Dale Collection

Library of Congress Cataloging-in-Publication Data

Wood, Alix.
 Camille Pissarro / Alix Wood.
    pages cm. — (Artists through the ages)
 Includes index.
ISBN 978-1-6153-3918-1 (pbk.)
ISBN 978-1-6153-3919-8 (6 pack)
ISBN 978-1-6153-3917-4 (library binding)
1. Pissarro, Camille, 1830-1903—Juvenile literature. 2. Painters—France—Biography—
Juvenile literature. I. Title.
 ND553.P55W66 2015
 759.4—dc23
 [B]

                                    2014028089

Manufactured in the United States of America

CPSIA Compliance Information: Batch #CW15WM: For Further Information contact Windmill Books, New York, New York at 1-866-478-0556

Contents

Who Was Pissarro?

Camille Pissarro was an **Impressionist** and **Postimpressionist** artist. He was considered an encouraging father-figure to many other artists during his painting career. He was born in 1830 on the island of St. Thomas which is now in the US Virgin Islands. His mother came from the island, and his father was a Portuguese businessman.

Camille Pissarro

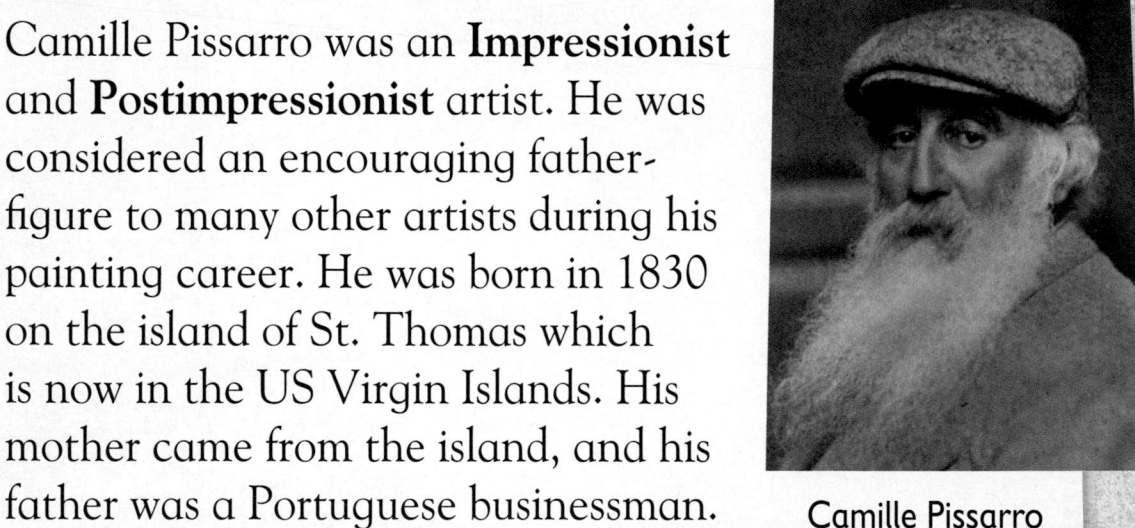

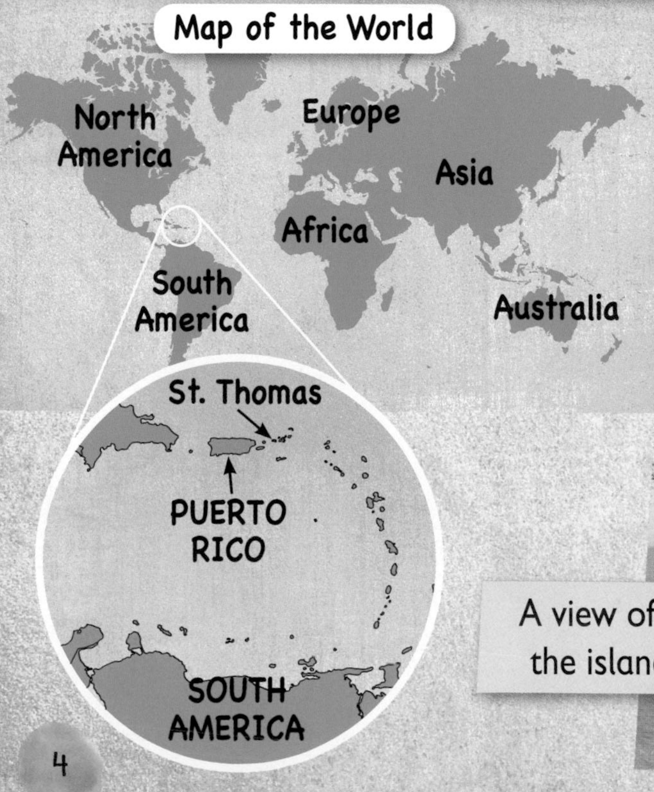

Map of the World

North America

Europe

Asia

Africa

South America

Australia

St. Thomas

PUERTO RICO

SOUTH AMERICA

A view of Magens Bay on the island of St. Thomas.

Pissarro's father was named Jacob. Jacob came to St. Thomas to help sort out the business affairs of his uncle, who had died. He fell in love, and married his uncle's **widow**. Some people on the island thought that this was wrong. When their children went to school they were not allowed to attend the Jewish school on the island, and were forced to go to the local school instead.

Boarding School and Work

When Pissarro was twelve he went to a boarding school near Paris, France. He loved studying art. His teacher, Monsieur Savary, encouraged him to become an artist when he left at age 17. His father wanted him to work for him as a cargo clerk in the busy port of Charlotte Amalie. Pissarro drew and painted in his spare time instead.

Charlotte Amalie is still a busy port today.

Painting St. Thomas

Pissarro took his teacher's advice and spent all his spare time painting. He liked to paint the daily lives of the people on St. Thomas.

Pissarro became friends with the Danish artist Fritz Melbye, who was living on St. Thomas. Melbye convinced Pissarro to paint full-time. Pissarro wrote his family a note and left with Melbye to live in Venezuela for two years and paint.

Two Women Chatting By The Sea, St. Thomas, 1856

Brothers

In 1855 Pissarro moved to Paris. He worked as an assistant to Fritz Melbye's brother, the painter Anton Melbye. Anton liked to paint stormy seas.

7

Artist Friends

In Paris, Pissarro went to an art school called the Académie Suisse. He made friends with many young artists, such as Claude Monet and Paul Cézanne. They painted people in natural settings, without any grandness. They disliked the old-fashioned galleries, such as the *Salon*. The *Salon* did not like their natural style and refused to exhibit their paintings!

Pissarro's painting *The Woods at Marly*, 1871, was typical of his new, natural style.

Pissarro married his mother's maid, Julie Vellay. They had eight children, but two of them died young. They lived outside Paris, first in Pontoise, and then at Louveciennes. Both places inspired many of Pissarro's paintings. Pissarro painted scenes of village life, the local landscape, and ordinary people at work.

Camille Pissarro with his wife Julie, 1877

A landscape by the Japanese artist Hokusai.

Japanese Art

Japanese art was popular in France in Pissarro's time. Japanese prints were often **asymmetrical**, with most detail on one side of a painting. They also usually had large areas of flat color. Pissarro experimented with this new way of composing a picture.

In London

In 1870, the outbreak of the Franco-Prussian War meant Pissarro, with Danish nationality, could not join the army. Instead, he moved his family to Norwood, a village on the edge of London.

Pissarro met up with his friend Claude Monet in London, and the Paris art dealer Paul Durand-Ruel. Durand-Ruel went on to help sell Pissarro's art for most of his life. Pissarro visited England several times during his life and painted many **landscapes**.

C. Pissarro. 1871

The Road To Sydenham. Painted during Pissarro's stay in London in 1871.

Back in France

When Pissarro returned to France after the war, things at home were not as he had left them. Of the 1,500 paintings that he had left behind, only around 40 were still at his home. The others had been damaged or destroyed by soldiers, who had even used some of them to wipe their boots on!

Pissarro rejoined his group of artist friends. Because the *Salon* still refused to exhibit their paintings, Pissarro suggested that they should set up their own society. In 1873, 15 artists set up a group, with Pissarro as a leading figure. The group went on to hold an exhibition each year for eight years. The group included artists such as Claude Monet, Auguste Renoir, Edgar Degas, and Alfred Sisley.

The Fence, 1872

In the early 1870s Pissarro painted in an Impressionist style. He liked to paint outside, and he would finish a painting in one day.

Pissarro's Group

His group was called the Association of Painters, Sculptors, and Engravers. The name "Impressionist" hadn't been thought of yet.

Impressionism

The Impressionist movement got its name from a painting Claude Monet exhibited called *Impression, Sunrise*. An **art critic** said the painting looked "half-finished" like all the works on show, and he called the group "Impressionists." It was meant as an insult, but the artists decided to adopt the name!

Durand-Ruel

Paul Durand-Ruel was a French art dealer who saw the importance of Impressionism. He sold many of Pissarro's and his group's paintings. The money allowed the artists to continue to paint.

Pissarro's friend Auguste Renoir painted this portrait of Paul Durand-Ruel in 1910.

Art critics did not like the new style of painting any more than the *Salon* had. They did not like what the artists chose to paint. They painted commonplace scenes featuring everyday people, instead of grand places and people. The paintings were thought to be sketchy and looked too unfinished. Critics did not like the visible brushstrokes that the artists used, either.

The Road from Versailles to Louveciennes, painted around 1872

Father Figure

Pissarro's group of Impressionist artists had very different personalities and ideas. The reason they stayed together as long as they did without major arguments was because of Pissarro and his calm nature. The other artists considered him a kind and patient father figure. He would take time to teach some of the other artists his methods. These lessons led to Cézanne changing his total approach to art.

Charing Cross Bridge, London, 1890

17

Orchard in Bloom

Orchard in Bloom, Louveciennes was at the top of Pissarro's list of paintings for the 1874 exhibition. When Pissarro returned to France after the war, it was to this house in Louveciennes, which had been occupied by soldiers. Pissarro waited a while before he could face going back to the house. *Orchard in Bloom, Louveciennes,* was painted the next spring. It is a painting full of beauty and hope for the future harvest. He sold the painting to Durand-Ruel.

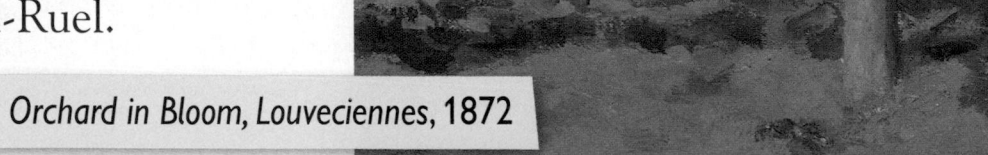

Orchard in Bloom, Louveciennes, 1872

C. Pissarro

19

Ordinary People

Most Impressionist painters painted rich people at leisure in their art, but Pissarro liked to paint country landscapes and farmworkers. He often put small figures into his landscapes, like in the painting *Hampton Court Green* below.

Hampton Court Green, 1891

People also became the main focus of the paintings. *Peasant Girl with a Straw Hat* is a portrait of a young woman resting during a day working in the fields. Her apron and hat would have protected her from the dirt and the sun while working.

Peasant Girl with a Straw Hat, 1881

A New Style

Pissarro developed a new style of applying paint. He used broad, single brushstrokes, and never used black for shadowed areas. In this painting strokes of green shade the woman's jaw and neck. Pissarro worked back in the **studio** to give a more finished, detailed look to these paintings.

Millet's Influence

A painter called Jean-François Millet painted ordinary people working in the fields a little before Pissarro started painting them. The difference between his work and Pissarro's was that Millet had a romantic view of farm laborers. Pissarro's paintings were considered new because he painted realistic settings, without trying to make the workers' lives look **idyllic** and romantic.

Millet focused on the dignity of hard work. As new machines were being used to do the jobs of people in the countryside, Millet was painting a disappearing way of life.

Man with Wheelbarrow, an etching by Millet, 1855

Honest Portraits

Pissarro's paintings were straightforward portraits of ordinary people at work. He made farm work appear important, which was unusual at the time.

The Gardener - Old Peasant with Cabbage, by Pissarro, was painted between 1883-1895

Seurat and Signac

In 1885 Pissarro met artists Georges Seurat and Paul Signac. Both artists used a way of painting called **pointillism** where dots of pure colors placed next to each other create the illusion of blended colors when viewed from a distance.

Pointillism

The diagram below shows how pointillism works. Only dots of the three primary colors, red, blue, and yellow, have been used. When dots are close to each other, your eyes mix the color.

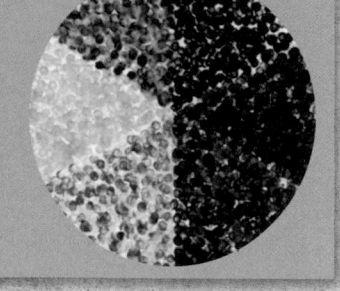

From 1885 to 1888 Pissarro tried this new way of painting. His work was very different from his Impressionist paintings. Pissarro was always happy to alter his style and try new techniques. Pissarro is believed to be the only Impressionist artist who also painted in the pointillist style, sometimes called **Neo-Impressionism**.

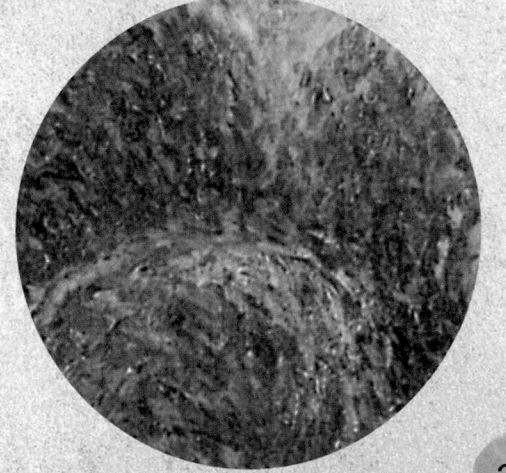

The Harvest of Hay in Eragny, 1887

This close-up of the hay in the painting *The Harvest of Hay in Eragny* shows the different-colored pointillist paint strokes clearly.

From Windows

As Pissarro got older he suffered from eye **infections** which stopped him being able to paint outdoors, except in warm weather. Because of this he began painting sitting at the window of his hotel room when he traveled. He often chose rooms on the top floor so that he could get a good view. He traveled around northern France and London staying in hotels and painting the scenes on the streets below him.

Boulevard des Italiens, Morning, Sunlight, 1897

Pissarro's Last Years

Durand-Ruel was struggling to sell Pissarro's pointillism paintings, and Pissarro began to lose enthusiasm for the style. He returned to a more Impressionist way of painting. He kept the pointillist style's bright colors and obvious brushstrokes, though.

The Artist's Garden at Eragny, 1898

Etchings

This self-portrait by Pissarro is an etching. An etching is when an image is scratched into a metal plate, and then prints are made by applying ink to the plate and pressing paper against it. This sad-looking portrait was made soon after his mother had died.

Self-Portrait, around 1890

Pissarro died in Paris on November 13, 1903, at age 73. While other artists are perhaps more famous for a particular style, he will be remembered for not being afraid of change and for experimenting with art. He was a father figure and guide to generations of painters. His kind personality and encouragement helped many fellow artists. His work can be found in some of the most important museums today.

Glossary

art critic
(ART KRIH-tik)
A person whose job is
to analyze and interpret
works of art.

asymmetrical
(ay-sih-MEH-trih-kuhl)
When both sides of
something are uneven
in size or shape.

idyllic (eye-DIH-lihk)
Simple, enjoyable,
and charming.

Impressionist
(im-PREH-shuh-nist)
An artist who
concentrates on the
impression of a scene
using unmixed primary
colors and small
brushstrokes to
simulate light.

infection
(in-FEK-shun)
Contamination by a
disease which leads
to illness.

landscapes
(LAND-skayps)
Pictures of natural
scenery.

Neo-Impressionism
(NEE-oh–im-PRE-shuh-nizm)
A style of art that sought to improve Impressionism by a systematic approach to color and form.

pointillism
(POYN-tih-lih-zihm)
A technique of Neo-Impressionist painting using tiny dots of various pure colors, which become blended when viewed.

Postimpressionist
(POHST-im-PREH-shuh-nist)
An artist who reacted against the naturalism of the impressionists.

studio (STOO-dee-oh)
The working place of an artist.

widow (WIH-doh)
A woman whose husband has died.

Websites

For web resources related to the subject of this book, go to:
www.windmillbooks.com/weblinks
and select this book's title.

Read More

Dickins, Rosie. *Impressionists* (Young Reading (Series 3). London: Usborne Publishing Ltd, 2009.

Raimondo, Joyce. *Picture This!: Activities and Adventures in Impressionism.* (Art Explorers). New York, NY: Watson-Guptill Publications Inc., 2004.

Venezia, Mike. *Camille Pissarro* (Getting to Know the World's Greatest Artists). New York, NY: Children's Press; 2004.

Index